EAGLE ROCK

The Memoirs of a Little Girl 1941-45

by
Lake Pylant Monhollon

illustrated by
George Ann Brock

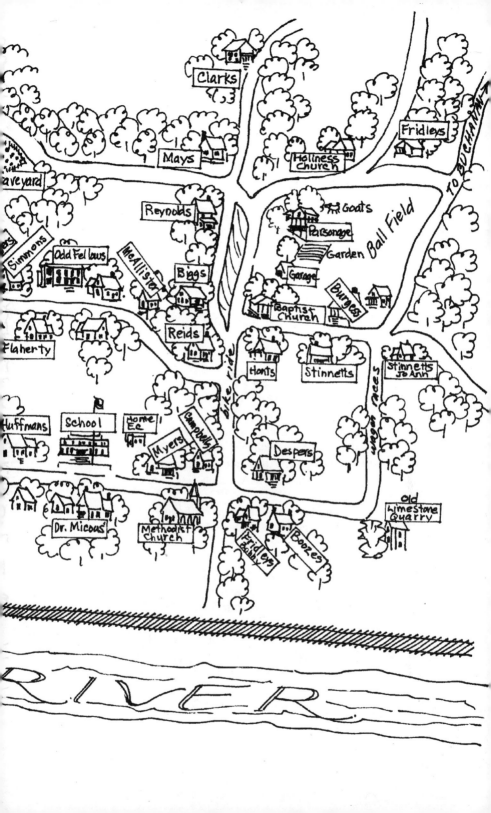

Copyright © 2003 by Reflection Publishing
Illustrations © 2003 by George Ann Brock
Book Design & Production by Imagination ii
Printed in U.S.A. All rights reserved.

Published by Reflection Publishing
1 Hendrick Drive, Abilene, Texas 79602
www.reflectionpublishing.com

Lake Pylant Monhollon
EAGLE ROCK
The Memoirs of a Little Girl 1941-45

Summary: A nostalgic look at a simpler day, when "things" were not so crucially important to the good life.

ISBN 0-9712142-1-2
LC 2003091483

Dedicated to Bill and Myrtie Simmons,
who still live in Eagle Rock and
who encouraged me to share
my "little girl" memories.

TABLE OF CONTENTS

1. First View 7
2. School 24
3. Entertainment 41
4. Main Street 66
5. Church 73
6. Our Animals 99
7. Camping 106
8. Health remedies 111
9. Chores 117
   Epilogue 125

1
First View

Mama pulled our '36 Chevy over to the curved shoulder of the road, saying, "Eagle Rock has to be close now. Let's look." My sister and I struggled out of the small car and stood by her side.

"O-o-h, Mama! This is it?" Looking down from that lofty curve, we saw Eagle Rock! A storybook picture in real life! A railroad track running alongside the James River edged the southern border of the small town. Houses peeped from among the trees on low hills in the river valley, and tall mountains stood on two sides. Cushioned among its many trees, the whole town was visible from our look-out on the curve. We had known that it wouldn't be a very big town (then at its peak population of 300 people), but this was better than I had dreamed!

The smallness of the town put it within the grasp of my six-year-old mind and imagination. It was *our* home, *our* town, *my* adventure! Daddy, whom we had not seen for weeks, would be there.

Mama exclaimed at the beauty of the view and then hustled my sister and me back into the car. Daddy was expecting us.

We drove across the James River Bridge (our very own bridge now, as I had claimed ownership) and turned right toward the town. Three old vine-covered kilns were the first landmarks to come into view. Of course, I had no idea what they were, but they looked grand and mysterious to me.

And then, there, right in the middle of the road was Daddy, smiling broadly and walking to meet us. Dear Daddy! Tall, thin, with black hair ruffling in the slight breeze, he ran over to the car as Mama brought it to a stop. She rolled down the window and held out her hand. He kissed her through the window, and then opened the door to reach into the back seat to hug me. My first words were, "See my new coat, Daddy? It has a velvet collar." My sister probably said something, too, but she didn't register much on my mind that day.

My mind raced ahead. I wanted to see our house, the parsonage, right away. Daddy must have read my mind.

"I'll bet my girls are eager to see their new home. It's big! I've been cleaning it, so I should know. It must have 150 windows! I have been washing them for days! It is only about a half mile from here to the church and our house." With that he climbed into the car next to Mama and directed our way, pointing out the homes of church members on the way.

"It's huge! It's big! It's…our house!" I breathed in awe, as I jumped out of the car. It was love at first sight for me when I saw that big

house. It really *was* big! I raced from room to room and up the stairs. I loved it, loved it! It sat on a high hill behind our big, beautiful church. (You think everything is big and high when you are a little person.) Exciting adventures were already forming in my imagination as I surveyed the house, the hill, the apple trees!

The church was absolutely stately and magnificent in my eyes, and I was so proud of Daddy for being its new pastor. I felt like the heroine in some story. (I was always the heroine in some story.)

Since there was still no furniture in the house, we spent several nights in the home of the Simmons. Mr. Simmons was probably the most prominent citizen of the town and chairman of the deacons at the church. Under the guidance of their daughter, Ruth, my sister and I toured the wonders of the town. The Noffsingers lived on this corner; the Despers lived on that corner and owned the funeral home; the Boozes and Fridleys were across from the Despers; the Reids lived on the side of the hill; the Burgesses lived next door to the church; another family of Fridleys were up the hill behind our house. Other neighbors were the Mays, the Reynolds, and the Biggs. The one doctor in town was red-haired, freckle-faced Dr. Micou.

Downtown consisted of a single street which hosted the Post Office, three grocery stores, a garage, and a bank. The railroad track ran parallel to this street, with the Depot on the other side of the tracks. A short train called the "Dinky" came through twice a day running from Clifton Forge to Lynchburg. Its coming and going was a big event for us kids.

My first trauma in Eagle Rock happened the second morning we were there. As I came down the stairs at the Simmons' house, Mr. Simmons greeted me with, "Did you know your daddy married a pretty blonde woman last night?"

"He did not," I declared stoutly.

"Yes, he did. He really did. She came over here after you went to bed, and he married her."

I expected grown people to be honest, and he was so serious, I felt tears rising up behind my eyes.

"He didn't. I know he didn't."

Fortunately, Mrs. Simmons came into the room at that moment and reassured me by finishing the tale, and my heart slowed down to a sensible rate.

"Don't worry, Patsy Lake. He's just teasing you. A couple came to the house last night to be married by our new preacher. Your daddy performed his first marriage ceremony right here in our living room."

Unfortunately, Daddy did not know he had to be bonded to marry people. When he found out the next morning, he rushed to the county seat, got the bond, hunted the couple down, and remarried them.

The day finally came for us to move into

our house. There were so many things in the big house that I had never seen before, and I was full of ooohs and aaahs and "what's this?" and "what's that?"

A closed-up fireplace was the focal point of the living room. Over the next four years Daddy married several couples in front of that fireplace. They would always pay him five dollars which he would give to Mama. She looked forward to that! He once did a double wedding, where twin sisters married twin brothers, and I peeked through the French doors.

A large pot-bellied stove took up one corner of Mama and Daddy's bedroom (the room that was supposed to be the dining room). There was a big wood/coal stove for cooking in the kitchen, and a smaller stove next to it for heating water. A short, oval, flat-topped stove stood in the center of the large bathroom upstairs. We were lucky to have an indoor bathroom. I would find out later that many of my friends did not have such a luxury.

A metal grate in the ceiling of the living room could be opened or closed to allow heat to go to the room above. Upstairs rooms, however, were seldom heated.

There were no closets. Daddy said,"I see that one of my first jobs will be to build frames for closets. And Mama will have to make curtains for the frames to hide our clothes."

By the way, clothes were a different kind of thing in Eagle Rock. They were different from my Austin clothes, partly because Mama had to make most of them on her treadle sewing machine.

But the material she used set them apart even more. Feed sacks! I didn't know feed sacks could be pretty, but they came in different colors and prints. Later, Mrs. McAllister, who taught Intermediates in our church, made several dresses for me to wear to school out of colored feed sacks. In fact, even my best church dress was feed-sack. Mama made my underwear from plain feed sacks.

Daddy showed my sister and me the cellar filled with coal and freshly cut wood. "You girls will have a job!" he said. "It will be your job to carry wood from the cellar for our stoves. I will carry the coal and build the fires."

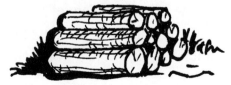

We would be able to take baths only on Saturdays, because Daddy would have to build two special fires for those occasions: one in the water-heating stove and another in the bathroom. Not taking baths very often became one of the big freedoms of Eagle Rock!

I had never seen a "wind-up" telephone before. We learned not to answer it every time it rang. We were on a party line. Our ring was one long and two shorts. There was no dial on the phone. Instead of dialing the way we had done in Austin, we would take the receiver off the hook, wind up the crank on the side, and when Central (the operator, Mrs. Biggs) answered, we would tell her whom we were calling. "Simmons residence, please." Or later, when Barbara West was my best friend, I would say, "Barbara West's residence, please."

My first girlfriend was Jo Ann Stinnett. She showed me other wonders of the town. A small creek ran under the road in front of the church, and the tunnel was almost too wonderful to believe.

Jo Ann lived on the second floor of an old, unpainted house. Her mother did a most unusual thing, I thought, giving us bread covered with butter and apple butter for a snack. It was my first experience with apple butter, and I really liked it! I savored every bite—though with a little nagging feeling of guilt in spite of the fact that a parent had given it to me. No one ate between meals in my home. It was unthinkable for a parent to let one eat between meals, especially anything sweet. Anyway, I felt very big and independent sitting in that tunnel, eating this new food, and talking to my new friend.

Jo Ann's mother was different in another way. She had a huge, huge stomach. I had never seen anyone shaped like that. Jo Ann explained that her mother was going to have a baby. That was nice, but I didn't connect that to her huge "stomach." There were so many things for little girls to learn, and Eagle Rock was full of them.

Another great thing about Eagle Rock was that I could walk anywhere in it. I had spent the first years of my life in Austin, Texas, a big city.

In Austin one could only go places in a car. This new town I could "own."

The most important place outside our home that I "owned" was the church. It was my church in a way the big church in Austin had never been. My daddy was the pastor of this church, and it was located at the bottom of our hill.

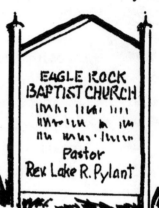

I was in Miss Lucy's Sunday School class, and I loved Miss Lucy (Mrs. Simmons). She always smiled. We had our own Sunday School quarterly with pictures to cut out and paste. Miss Lucy kept her hands clasped on the table in front of her while she told us Bible stories. Her two thumbs whirled around each other as she talked. I was almost hypnotized, watching her thumbs twirl. She taught us to put on our "golden gloves." As we pulled the imaginary

gloves onto each finger, we would say one word of the Golden Rule, ending with snapping them at our wrists on the words "unto....you." I think she had to rephrase it a bit to make it work: "Do unto others as you would that they should do....unto....you." (Matt. 7:12)

When Mama, with a hat perched atop her head, began to play "Loyalty to Christ" on the piano, classes came to a quick close and we filed into the sanctuary. I always sat on the very front row with my friend Barbara West. Sometimes, as Daddy preached, she and I would whisper as we thumbed through the hymn book or folded notebook paper into accordion fans.

One Sunday morning we got too loud. Daddy stopped his sermon, looked at me and said in a stern voice, "Patsy Lake."

I froze in my seat; my face flamed hot; my heart almost stopped. I didn't move during the rest of the sermon. I felt totally shamed as I left the church building that day. I wished that no one would say anything about it, but Mr. Simmons did. He often said things to me in teasing, but I took them very seriously. Daddy never mentioned it again. My parents were very good about forgetting such things. Punishment for disobedience came quickly and then they forgot it. I didn't.

My life revolved around the churches—five churches. Daddy was pastor of a field of five churches. They had beautiful names: Eagle Rock, Forest Grove, Longdale, Iron Gate, and Sharon. Later, when the field was divided, we kept Eagle Rock, Forest Grove, and Longdale.

Sunday dinners in Eagle Rock (and Longdale and Forest Grove) were grand affairs. Someone always invited the preacher's family over for dinner. Sometimes it took such a long time to serve the meal, I would almost despair. In farm homes they often waited until after church before they even killed the chicken. But I forgot all the agony when I saw the loaded table. I would eat until I hurt.

There would always be meat of some kind and a dessert, two things we rarely had at our house. I would look at Daddy as they passed out the dessert. He would nod, so I joyfully accepted it. My very favorite in all the world was lemon meringue pie with its high top of frothy meringue. The higher the top, the better I liked it.

Sometimes at the country churches in the summer, we would have dinner on the grounds. Everyone brought food and put it on a long table made of boards. It seemed to take an awfully long time to get this going, too. Sometimes we kids had to wave the flies off until we could get started. The adults went through the line first, getting the choicest pieces of chicken, but there was always far too much food, anyway. I was usually too full to eat another bite when it was time for dessert, but I ate one anyway, and then suffered.

I did not think it strange at the time that we ate only vegetables at home. Daddy put in a vegetable garden in the spring that supplied our needs throughout the year, thanks to Mama's canning. Some people thought it strange that we ate this way. It was quite satisfactory for Daddy, but Mama would have liked something more. The truth was that Daddy's salary was very small. Even in 1941, thirteen hundred dollars a year was not much. When we arrived in Eagle Rock, all five churches were "on the Board," meaning they could not support themselves without the help of the Virginia Baptist Board. During Daddy's four year pastorate, the three churches he kept after the field was divided would come off the Board.

On several occasions the people in the churches "pounded" us. That meant that we came home some Sunday evenings to find pounds of food on our table: fresh meat at hog-butchering time, canned foods, flour, sugar, fresh butter, and eggs. It was always more food than I could imagine we could ever eat.

I certainly did not know we were poor. I felt as if we were the elite of town, and in a sense we were. The pastor was a much respected person. Besides, no one in Eagle Rock was rich. Mr. Desper, the undertaker, might have been better off than most. Mr. Simmons did quite well, too. He owned the garage and worked on cars there. He also owned part of Myers grocery store.

2
School

My school career got off to a scary start. Daddy felt the call to be a pastor just as I reached the pivotal age of six. While he was looking for a church in Virginia, Mama took my sister and me to Daddy's hometown of Purvis, Mississippi. Through the last weeks of summer he preached at churches "in view of a call". September came and we were still in Purvis, so that is where my formal schooling began.

One happy day Daddy called to tell Mama about the "fine church" to which he had been called. She was so excited that she ran out into the street wearing her apron, waving the butcher knife in her hand, and calling the news to whoever was in hearing distance. Later, she learned that he had said "five" churches, not "a fine church."

That phone call marked our last day of school in Purvis. Mama threw our bags into the small trunk of our black Chevrolet and we were off to Virginia.

As we drove to our house that first day in Eagle Rock, we passed the big brick school in the center of town. It housed all eleven grades. (There were only eleven grades in Virginia schools at that time.) Any activities that did not take place in the churches took place at the school, though these were few. Once, a cowboy singing group came and performed on the stage that was on one side of the basketball court. Chairs were set up on the basketball court. I fell totally in love with "Smiley." Everyday the next week I tried to find his program on the radio.

Since the Eagle Rock school was already in full swing, Mama took me to meet my teacher, Miss Flaherty in front of a full classroom. Miss Flaherty said I would be in the primer group. After setting the class to work, Miss Flaherty called me up to her desk, where she had several primer readers. She asked me which one I had started on in Mississippi. I didn't know, but I hated to say so. None of her books looked familiar. She would open one book, and I would look at the page and recognize nothing. She held up book after book. By the time we reached the last book, I felt my heart pounding hard and my face getting hot, so I said, "This one." Then I had to bear the embarrassment of appearing dumb, because she had to tell me every word. Fortunately, I was a fast learner. I don't remember being taught phonics. I think I just memorized all the words as I went along.

After spending a few days sitting at a table with several children, Miss Flaherty sent me to a large double desk where another girl was already sitting. Having a desk partner was a good thing, as we could help each other. When we had to put our heads down on the desk for rest time, she and I would play pencil games on the seat between us.

The teacher divided us into groups for reading time. While one group sat around a table and read to her, the other groups worked at their spelling or arithmetic assignments.

At the reading table with my group, I sat next to Bobby Fridley. He read with a loud voice. But the strangest thing about Bobby was that he always smelled like Ivory soap. I thought that no one took daily baths in Eagle Rock! I think his mother must have washed his face and ears every morning.

I was able to be more sympathetic with Bobby after our Aunt Yuba came to visit one time. Mother had gone to Florida to be with her father, who was seriously ill. So Daddy's sister, Yuba, came from Mississippi to stay with us.

Aunt Yuba introduced Sister and me to one shock after another. The first shock came on her first morning with us. "Okay, Girls, wash your face, neck, and ears, and do it well," she said as she placed two pans of water, a bar of soap, and two washrags on the living room floor.

I couldn't believe my ears! She was telling us to wash! We told her we never did that, but it didn't matter to her. So we sat down on the floor and washed. Every morning we washed.

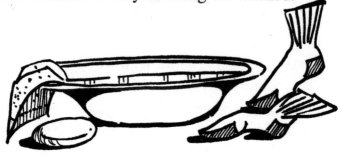

The next shock came in the afternoon when we returned from school. There was a pan of sudsy water sitting on the stove with our socks in it. We were expected to wash out our own socks! It seemed that Aunt Yuba stayed with us for a long, long time.

Recess was wonderful. My new girlfriends and I raced down the outside steps onto the playground. We had a totally free, unsupervised playtime. We made up our own games. Jumping rope was a big favorite for the girls. Two would turn the rope and the rest of us would "run through," or take turns, or several at a time would do the rhymes.

"Red, white, *and* blue,..."

Then the rope turners would turn the rope high over our heads as we stooped and chanted,

"Stars are shining over *you*."

Standing up again on the "you," we would count off the jumps, "One, two, three......" until we missed.

A short, but challenging jump was "Teddy Bear."

"Teddy Bear, Teddy Bear, turn around;
Teddy Bear, Teddy Bear, touch the ground;
Teddy Bear, Teddy Bear, tie your shoe,
Teddy Bear, Teddy Bear, that will do."

And with that we would run out of the rope and the next person would run in.

Of course, there was "Hot Pepper" when the turners turned the rope as fast as they could.

"Mabel, Mabel, set the table,
Don't forget the salt and **pepper**...."

The boys, and sometimes the girls, too, played marbles. I began a great collection of marbles, with an extra large one I called Jupiter (as soon as I learned about that largest planet). Jupiter was my shooter.

We would draw a circle in the hard dirt with a stick and each person would place a certain number of his ordinary marbles inside. Then, crouching down on the ground we would aim and fire our shooter marble into the ring, each of us trying to knock the most marbles out of the ring. (The firing was done by flipping our thumb against the marble held in our curled index finger.) If we were playing for "keeps," we could keep all the marbles we knocked out. I didn't like to play for keeps, because I had named all my marbles and wanted to keep my own.

Making friends was pretty easy. Being the daughter of the new Baptist preacher in a very small town meant automatic recognition and attention. I wore my hair in pigtails that became my trademark. I always, always wore pigtails.

I was usually the leader in any game that needed leaders. If it was the kind of game where the leaders had to choose their teams and I didn't happen to be the leader, the leader would choose me early on. The leader would choose the first one or two players for ability and then would pick her friends. My only hope was to be picked on the "friend basis." I was not very good at anything physical, but I faked it as best I could. Spelling bees were another matter. I always won the spelling bees.

When the teacher assigned clean-up jobs in the classroom, the prize job was dusting the erasers. "Me," "Me," "Choose me," a cacophony of voices sang out. The two lucky ones gathered up the erasers from the ledges of the blackboards and walked importantly to the outside of the building. We pounded them till the chalk dust flew and white marks covered the red brick wall. When no more dust would come out of them, we gave it up and went back in.

Sometimes I ran home for lunch, but more often I brought my lunch in a "poke." In the mountains of Virginia a poke was a paper sack. After eating my sandwich and apple, I carefully folded my poke to take home. These were the years of World War II and pokes were hard to come by.

My teacher in second grade was Miss Austin. In third grade it was Mrs. Nabors. In fourth grade it was Mrs. Woods. But the kids were always the same. There was just one class for each grade.

When it came time for typhoid shots, panic seized my usually intrepid heart. Everyone in school walked across the street to Dr. Micou's office to get the shot. I was absolutely terrified, and we got the shots not once, but three weeks in a row! The misery did not end when the shot was over each week. The next day my arm would be so sore, I could not stand for anyone to touch it. And someone always did. If no one touched it deliberately, jostling kids bumped it in the hallway.

Doctors scared me terribly anyway.

Someone decided everyone in school should have his tonsils out. The principal drove a school bus full of kids to Roanoke to have them out. Thank goodness, Daddy wouldn't hear of it for me.

"God gave you tonsils for a reason, Patsy Lake, and you should keep them as long as you can," he said.

I felt sorry for the other kids who had to go. I felt even sorrier for them when they came back and couldn't swallow. I didn't care if they did get ice cream.

Ice cream was a treat I did not get very often. On the rare occasions Daddy let me have an ice cream cone, I had to use my own nickel. I got a quarter each week for an allowance starting in the second grade, a real splurge on his part. A friend and I would run down to Rudisills grocery store, since it was the only place in town that had ice cream.

"A one-dip cone of raspberry sherbet, please," I told Mr. Rudisill, holding out my nickel. Double dips were a dime, so we never got one of those.

By the time I finished the second grade, I discovered Nancy Drew. The first Nancy Drew book I read was *The Secret at Shadow Ranch*. It took me a long time to read it, because I was a slow reader. But I stayed with it. I was totally, totally absorbed in it every free moment.

I would read until my eyes were ready to drop out. (By now I was wearing glasses to read.) Daddy would say, "Patsy Lake, stop reading and rest your eyes." So I would put down my book and impatiently wait for my eyes to rest.

I borrowed all the Nancy Drew books that were in our school library and borrowed them from anyone in town who had one. Then when I had exhausted all those resources, I began to save my money in earnest. Out of my twenty-five cent allowance each week, I gave five cents to the church and saved the rest for books.

On the infrequent occasions when Mama and Daddy (or Mama and Miss Lucy) drove to Roanoke, I took my savings in my zipper billfold and climbed into the back seat. (I thought it was a great billfold because it had a map of the United States on the front and a list of the Presidents on the back.)

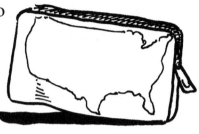

After parking, Mama would let Sister and me go wherever we wanted, just so she knew where. I hurried immediately to Pugh's Department Store and went to their book section. There would be a whole row of Nancy Drew books! I counted out my sixty cents to the lady and hugged my new book to my chest. At that point I was through with shopping and ready to go home.

Usually Mama was not ready to go so soon and would park Sister and me at a picture show. (My sister's name was Rose Melody, but I always called her "Sister.") Mama must have thought one show was as good as another, because she would park us at some of the awfulest, scariest movies there were. One time it was a double-header: "I Walked with a Zombie" and "The Revenge of the Zombies." Another time it was "The Wizard of Oz." We spent much of our time hiding our heads behind the seat in front of us. Sometimes Mama would let us sit through the shows twice.

My favorite picture shows were the jungle ones, with Hedy Lamar or Dorothy Lamour and Bob Hope. One movie that scared me to death, but was terribly funny, too, was "Topper Returns." I would get a lot of mileage out of that one, telling it to friends. "Henry Aldridge Haunts a House" terrified me very much at the time, but it gave me a lot to think about and a lot to build stories on later.

One of my greatest talents in those days was storytelling. When there was time at the end of class and we were waiting for the bell to ring, kids would say, "Let Patsy tell a story." If there was time, the teacher would usually let me. No one ever knew when the bell would ring, so I just told the story until it rang. My stories were very long, and would continue from day to day. I made them up as I went along, drawing on one of the movies I had seen, a story I had heard, or just my imagination. Often the hero of my story would be a baby who could do all kinds of impossible things.

During third grade, I discovered other books. It was really hard for me to break over from one series to another, and it took a lot of persuasion to convince me that any book that was not a Nancy Drew would be any good. But the Dana Girls actually rivaled Nancy Drew. They were so good I could hardly stand it.

Sister could whip through a book in a day, but I would take many days, digesting every word, every thought, every picture.

Judy Boltons weren't nearly as good, but when hard up for one of my favorite series, I would read a Judy Bolton. In the fourth grade, I had to switch to Hardy Boys, because I had drained our small library of everything else in the way of mystery series. I could not save money fast enough to buy many, and besides, we did not get to go to Roanoke often.

I treasured every book, even my school books. We had to go to a special school book store in Roanoke to get our books and Mother and Daddy paid for them. It was so exciting to see those new books stacked up and handed to me by the clerk. It wasn't nearly as good if I had to take a secondhand one. As I sat and turned the pages, I breathed deeply of that new smell, looked at the clean, fresh pages, and felt the smooth new cover. Secondhand books had a different kind of charm. They looked "experienced," and had an old book smell. I didn't sell my books at the end of the year, except the secondhand ones. The new ones became a part of my library.

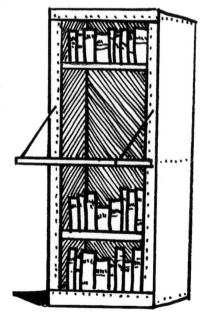

Daddy built me a desk out of a coffin box. He built desks for himself and mama out of coffin boxes, too, and built a storage closet out of one. Since Mr. Desper, the undertaker, was in our church, he gave us the boxes.

Daddy used red thumb tacks to cover the outside of my desk with white oil cloth. The inside writing surface was linoleum. There was a hinged door that could close up this writing area. Underneath, there were two shelves for my precious books.

I wrote my name in each book and if I lent one out, I never forgot who had it. I began to visualize a lending library of my own. I imagined how I would arrange the shelves and how I would check out the books the way the school librarian did. However, other kids were not as careful with books as I was, and when they tore a jacket, I was so grieved I gave up my idea of a lending library. In my library, I would just handle the books, rearrange the books, and look at them.

Daddy tried to get me interested in the faded, dusty-looking series of historical novels inherited from Mama's dad. But the print was so tiny, and they were thick and dull-looking. The one picture in the front just didn't have enough power to overcome all that. Besides the pictures didn't even look interesting. They were pictures of women in long dresses and men in odd-looking suits.

Poor Daddy! He tried to interest me in those books more than once. He didn't have time to read them, and I think he thought they were going to waste.

3
Entertainment

"I get the good stool!" "I get to be the closest!" Sister and I shrieked as we raced to the radio that sat on a shelf in the pantry. Every Saturday morning, at the magic moment, Sister and I perched in front of the radio to hear "Let's Pretend." The commercial for Cream of Wheat became my Saturday theme song.

"Cream of Wheat is so good to eat,
Yes, we have it every day.
We sing this song for it makes you strong
And it makes you shout,
 'Hooray.'
It's good for growing babies, and grown-ups too, to eat;
For all the family's breakfast, you can't beat Cream of Wheat."

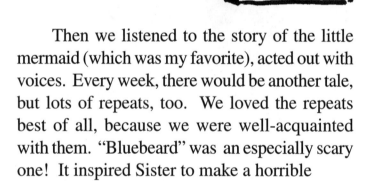

Then we listened to the story of the little mermaid (which was my favorite), acted out with voices. Every week, there would be another tale, but lots of repeats, too. We loved the repeats best of all, because we were well-acquainted with them. "Bluebeard" was an especially scary one! It inspired Sister to make a horrible

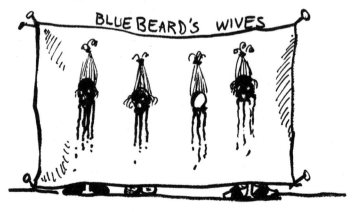

Bluebeard booth at one of our Halloween parties. Girls stuck their heads through a "bloody" sheet, letting them dangle from their pinned-up hair, like the heads of Bluebeard's wives.

Reading was my favorite entertainment during the rest of the week. What joy when Sister and I discovered stacks and stacks of comic books at the Simmons' house! Billy and Frank were away at war, but we found their bedroom on the second floor, clean and neat and empty. And cold. Not a place to attract kids—except for their closet! We would sit on the floor of that closet next to the stacked comic books and read until it was time to go home. What a treasure trove! As soon as we finished a big Sunday dinner at their house, the two of us would head for that closet. We would read comics until my eyes were exhausted. (I always read to exhaustion.)

Later on, Daddy decided that we shouldn't read comics on Sunday. One day when he was visiting for the church, he told a little boy in the household, "I hope you will be in church tomorrow for Sunday School." Daddy was startled by the response: "Oh, boy, tomorrow is Sunday! Tomorrow is Sunday funnies day!" Daddy thought it was terrible for someone to look

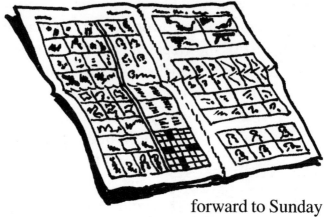

forward to Sunday just so he could read the funny papers. From then on, he would always hide the Sunday newspaper until Monday.

If I was not reading, or if I was resting my eyes, I might go climb my favorite apple tree, which was at the bottom of the hill behind the garage. There were several apple trees on our hill, but this one was shaped for climbing. The bottom limb was smooth and easy to reach. It twisted back over another limb to form the "sitting room." Higher limbs were the bedroom and kitchen. Sometimes friends would join me in the tree.

One day when the apples were getting ripe, Virginia Ann Burgess and I picked a basket of apples, washed and polished them until they looked artificial, and went from door to door trying to sell them. People didn't buy them, so we ate them, and that evening I had a terrible stomachache.

Daddy said, "You ate too many artificial apples, Patsy Lake."

The front steps of the church were bordered with beautiful, heavily blooming hollyhocks.

They made the church look good and were a great source of creative activity for kids.

We would take off a flower, turn it upside down and make a girl doll in a long dress. Her head was a peeled bud that actually had eyes. We pressed it down onto the piece of stem that was left sticking up on the shoulders of the "dress." In their beautifully colored gowns they made attractive residents of the maple tree towns described below.

There were huge maple trees in our front yard. Not only were they pretty and good sources of shade, they also offered a lot of entertainment. The limbs were far too high for climbing, but some of them bent over far enough for us to pick leaves that were big and flat and soft and just right for making "clothes." We would pinch the stem off to use as a pin, and then pin the leaves together into skirts and vests.

One game that would occupy my friends

and me for hours was building a town beneath one of our big maple trees where there was no grass and where the roots were big. We would scrape out roads and driveways and arrange rocks for houses and twigs for trees. Our hollyhock dolls in their beautifully colored gowns made attractive residents. Match boxes had to serve as cars. None of us owned a real toy car.

No one owned a real wagon either, but oh, the wonderful wagons the boys built. The only place I had ever seen a store-bought red wagon was in the Sears Roebuck catalog, but it didn't look nearly as good as the ones my friends built. They scavenged wheels from anywhere they could find them. They used a long board for the body with cross boards that swiveled for axles. A bushel basket lid might be the seat, and a rope was attached to the front axle board to guide it.

The boys raced the wagons down the road leading to the abandoned limestone quarry.

I know the abandoned limestone quarry sounds interesting, but it wasn't much of an attraction to us kids. Adults, of course, had cautioned us against going into the old building at the quarry, but I think the main deterrent was that deep white lime dust covered everything, and it was not pleasant to walk through.

Another favorite game was "store." We could set up the most elaborate stores. Some days it was a grocery store. Everyone would bring cans and boxes they had salvaged from the trash cans at home. We built counters with shelves behind them to hold the groceries. The "shopper" would come with her basket and read off her purchases as she surveyed the shelves to see what was available. The "clerk" would write the items down on a pad, reach back on the shelf to get them, and figure up the total

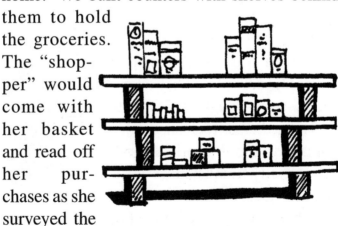

owed. Usually the groceries had to be returned before the next customer could shop.

The thing that endeared the game to me was the spice cans that some kids brought. Our mother never used spices, so I was enthralled with the little cinnamon, allspice, and nutmeg cans. That is all I ever wanted to buy, so I could take off the lids and breathe that unbelievable smell. After the game was over, the kids would casually throw those cans away, but if I could, I would squirrel some away for another day of shopping, or just as a treasure.

One day Sister and Virginia Reynolds, who lived across the road from us, put together a whole department store in the large entrance hall and up the stairs of the parsonage. It took them hours to arrange all the dresses in one section, shoes in another, and hats on the stair landing— all of which were Mama's clothes. At my insistence, they put in a book section. By the time the store was all set up, everyone was too tired to play. Oh, well. It had been fun to set up the store. Somehow or another we never thought of the next logical step: putting everything away.

Mama reminded us. That wasn't so much fun.

It was not until I was in the fourth grade that someone in town got a bicycle. George Burgess, who lived next door to the church at the bottom of our hill, got a brand new bicycle. The whole town of kids flocked daily in front of his house, hoping to get a turn at riding.

I didn't know how to ride, of course, but he took the time to hold the bike so I could get my balance. As I practiced that day, he walked along beside me in front of the church. Then we turned on the road by the Honts' house. When he thought I was going good, he turned me loose. Unfortunately, the road turned down at a pretty good slope and I found myself sailing toward the Methodist Church on the corner.

Panic is too mild a word to describe my terror. I could never make the turn at the corner! Everyone was screaming, "Put on your brakes! Put on your brakes!" What brakes? No one had told me about brakes. I almost stopped breathing as I clutched the handlebars. I knew the End was near. Miraculously, the bicycle made a smooth, wide-arching turn, the bike lost speed and George and Sister caught up with me, catching the bike before it went over.

Everyone was saying, "Wow! You can ride! How did you make the turn going so fast?" I didn't know. I was full of wonder about that, myself. But I was very, very grateful. I also knew that was enough bicycle business for me that day, and made my way home on wobbly, rubber legs.

The only toys I ever owned, except for marbles and jacks, were my dolls—Sammy, Judy June and Lucy Louise. Of course, these I only owned one at a time. Sammy was a rubber di-dy (dye-dee) that rotted away. I loved this kind of doll because I could give it a bottle of water that ran through it and wet its diaper. Judy

June, also a di-dy doll, took his place. Gama, my grandmother on Mama's side, made a small suitcase of clothes for Judy June. I changed her diapers

and dressed her. But in spite of my good care, her little rubber body did not last long, rotting from the water that was always inside her. Sammy and Judy June were named after some of my favorite people in Austin—Sam and June Bills.

My next doll was named after Lucy Simmons and Louise Honts of Eagle Rock. Lucy Louise was a different kind of doll. She was bigger and had a cloth body with wooden legs and head, and eyes that opened and closed and rolled sideways.

I can still feel the wonder and awe of the moment when I first saw her in the early morning of our second Christmas in Eagle Rock! My eyes must have been as big and round as hers as I marveled over the beautiful doll.

Mama had made a bassinet out of a cardboard box that she had covered with white flannel and pink ribbons and a net skirt. Lucy Louise was sitting up in the bassinet, wearing her pink store-bought dress and bonnet. Hanging over the side of the bassinet were two more dresses that Mama had made—a blue flowered dotted Swiss, edged with rick-rack and a soft white dress with tucks at the neck.

The most wonderful piece of clothing Mama had made was a baby bunting. The bunting was made of soft white flannel, edged with pink ribbon. One corner of it gathered into a hood with a ribbon to hold it on. When I wrapped the bunting around the doll, it showed pretty pink and blue and green flowers that Mama had embroidered.

I had several friends who liked to play dolls.

We would dress them (with me nearly always wrapping mine in the bunting) and take them places with us.

The Burgesses had a little sister named Betty Sue who tore her dolls up. I could not believe the ugly naked broken dolls with their eyes hanging out! We kept our dolls out of Betty Sue's reach.

I also loved paper dolls. I had such beautiful ones: Jeannette MacDonald in her billowing long skirts, Hedy Lamar in sarongs, Sonja Henie in ice skating outfits. These were my only real paper dolls for years. Since there was a war going on, paper dolls were all but unavailable. There was the paper shortage and everyone was too busy building guns and airplanes and necessities to make something like paper dolls.

Mama drew some for me on notebook paper, but the dolls were disappointingly flimsy and had blue lines on them. Sometimes there were paper dolls in the comic section of the Sunday newspaper, though, and they were treasures!

The store-bought paper dolls had perforated edges. I could just pop them out of the cardboard covers of the paper doll book. I had to cut each dress out with scissors. After cutting out all the dresses, I put them in their separate piles and dressed the dolls for the different activities my friends and I invented for them.

The song "Paper Doll" was a popular war song and I knew every word.

> "I'm goin' to buy a paper doll that I can call my own.
> A doll that other fellows cannot steal.
> And then those flirty, flirty guys with their flirty, flirty eyes
> Will have to play with dollies that are real.
> When I come home at night she will be waiting.
> She'll be the truest girl in all the world.
> I'd rather have a paper doll to call my own
> Than have a fickle-minded real live girl."[1]

---

[1] Black, Johnny S. "Paper Doll," c1915. E.B. Marks (publisher), c1942.

Sister collected sheet music the way I collected books, and she learned to play the music on the piano. We learned all the popular war-time songs.

We had many sing-songs around the piano in the evenings. Usually, Mama played, I sat by her, and Sister and Daddy stood behind us. We sang hymns, and sometimes Mama would play the popular songs for us, too.

Daddy thought the song, "Huggin' and Chalkin'" was a bad one. It was the cover of the sheet music that he didn't like, I think. It showed a man hugging a fat woman and making X's in white chalk on her back.

"Gee, but ain't it grand to
have a girl so big and fat
That when you go to hug her, you don't know where you're at,
You have to take a piece of chalk in your hand
And hug a ways and chalk a mark to see where you began...."[2]

The song ends with the fellow hugging and

---

[2] Hayes, Clarence Leonard and Goell, Kermit. "Huggin' and Chalkin'," c1946.

chalking his way around his girl one day when he ran into a guy coming around the other way. I thought it was funny—but what did I know?

Sunday afternoons, a bunch of us kids took long walks up the road toward Buchanan. Sometimes, in the winter when the trees were bare, we would walk through the woods, shuffling through leaves. The thought of snakes never came to mind and, fortunately, we never saw one. We would walk until we were too tired to walk further, and then realize we had to walk all the way back. So short-sighted, yet we never did learn to turn around before exhaustion set in.

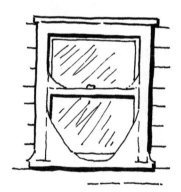

In the winter, snow added a whole new dimension to playtime. Nothing was quite so wonderful as looking out the window in the morning to see the ground covered with a fresh blanket of snow! Oh, the wonders *that* opened up! Of course, school was called off, because the buses could not run.

Almost before we could finish breakfast, kids would begin arriving at our back door, which opened onto the best sledding hill in town. Everyone was bundled up beyond recognition, and we hurried to do likewise.

With Mama's help we put on layer after layer, including thick snow pants. As we came out the door, some sleds were already cruising down the slope. Others were having their runners "greased" with parafin.

The first time we brought out our new sleds, Frank Simmons, who hadn't gone to war yet, helped us sand the painted finish off the bottom of our runners. He said they would never go with that paint on them. He sanded them and waxed them, while we waited impatiently to join the others.

I rushed to get into line and sat down on my sled. Then, all of a sudden I wasn't in such a rush. This was a high hill. "How do you guide this thing?" I asked.

"Lie down on the sled and guide it with your hands," Frank shouted above the kids' screams. He put my hands on the steering bar, and I was off.

Oh, it was great, great! Quite worth the long climb back up the hill, pulling the sled by the rope he had attached to it. Again and again, I went down the hill. My nose got colder and colder, and soon I began wiping it with my mittened hand. My hands were getting cold, too, but I slid on and on, feeling this was the greatest of all adventures.

Daddy built a big bonfire at the top of the hill so we could warm up a bit, and that added to the excitement of it all. Daddy liked to sled, too, so Sister and I had to share our sleds with him from time to time. Or sometimes he would let us go down on his back.

I eventually felt brave enough to sit up on

the sled and guide it with my feet. That was far better yet.

Finally, everyone began to take breaks or go home for lunch. I staggered through our back door into the kitchen with frozen face and hands. Mama helped me get out of all my layers, hanging my mittens to dry near the stove. The warmth of the kitchen stove began to thaw my frozen parts, and they stung and burned as they thawed.

Then suddenly I realized I was very, very tired. I stayed tired just long enough to eat the hot soup Mama had fixed, and then I was bundling up again, pulling on the almost-dry mittens.

The morning scene was repeated in the afternoon.

The second day of the snow Mama sent us out with a pan to get fresh snow to make snow ice cream. We had to hunt for a spot that hadn't been trampled, or traversed by a cat or dog. Then we scraped off the top layer with our bare hands and scooped up the clean snow beneath it. Mama added milk, sugar, and vanilla flavoring to the snow in the pan, and we had snow ice cream.

Gama thought up one of the most interesting games for us to play when Sister and I were both sick with the chicken pox. She showed us a scrapbook that her sister, Aunt Callie, had made when she was a girl, using old magazines and catalogs to furnish the rooms of a house. The pictures were yellowed with age, but the old-timey living room, dining room, kitchen, and other rooms were so attractive! It did look like a lot of fun.

Gama had brought with her from Florida two scrapbooks with paper covers. She got us settled on the floor by our daytime sick beds in the living room, with old catalogs, scissors, and paste. We hunted through the catalogs looking for appropriate sofas, chairs, curtains, etc. to furnish our rooms. It was hard to find furniture that did not have the price written on it, marring it, but Sister managed to make beautiful rooms. She had a flair for decorating, I guess, and I didn't. She put in extra little touches that never occurred to me. Also, she seemed to get to all the good pictures first. I copied her as much as I could.

In a way our scrapbooks were much prettier than Aunt Callie's, because our pictures were colored. But Aunt Callie's seemed so perfect. Sister's did, too.

I think the most fun game that kids played in the summer was tick-tacking. All it required was a nail, a long piece of string, and a piece of hardened resin. I never knew where they got the resin, but I treasured the one piece that I somehow acquired.

To prepare for tick-tacking, we would tie the string to the nail, sneak up to a house and push the nail up under one of the overlapping siding boards of the house, and hide a safe distance away. (Tick-tacking had to be done in the gloom of evening or after dark to be sure people were at home and to make hiding easier.)

From the hiding place we would draw the resin over the string as we tightened the tension on it. It would make a loud sawing noise that could be heard plainly inside the house.

The kids tick-tacked Sister and me in our bedroom once when Aunt Yuba was staying with us. She had made us go to bed even before dark, because the clock said bedtime even though it was summer and still light outside. We especially liked the tick-tacking that evening, because we knew the kids hadn't forgotten us.

But the best tick-tacking ever was the time I joined with a couple of friends to tick-tack the Reynolds across the road from us. It was dark and we hid behind a bush only a few feet away from the lighted window where Mr. Reynolds was sitting, listening to his radio.

Our resin was just right, and the sawing sound was the loudest I had ever heard. But Mr. Reynolds didn't seem to hear. He just kept on sitting there, listening to his radio. We continued to saw away. In a few minutes, he stood up, stretched, and walked out of the room. We were so disappointed, we decided we might as well go elsewhere.

Just at that moment, Mr. Reynolds sprang from the other side of the bush, dashing at us in a mad, crazy way. We threw our ball of string in the air and ran in all directions, with him in hot pursuit. Baby Mays and I fled under a clothesline where a large rug was hanging. Chickens squawked in loud terror at being awakened and dashed crazily under

our feet. Mr. Reynolds continued chasing us, yelling and swinging his arms like a wild man, till we were clear out of his yard. Then he turned and went back into his house.

Collecting ourselves in the road in front of

his house, we began to laugh. We laughed till we rolled in the road, as each one told his reaction to the sudden assault and what he had done. I thought that was the most fun I had ever had in my life! Mr. Reynolds never mentioned the episode to anyone or acted as if anything extraordinary had happened. But it was very extraordinary to us kids.

4
Main Street

I was often the one Mama sent to the store for small grocery items. Before I tell you about the stores, I need to tell you how nice I thought it would be if I had one of those little cars I saw in the toy section of the Sears Roebuck catalog. I could imagine myself driving one of those little cars to Myers' store, putting the groceries in the back seat and driving home. I didn't realize those cars had pedals like those on a tricycle, and that pedaling that car would have been more trouble than walking.

The Sears Roebuck and Montgomery Ward catalogs played several important roles in our lives during these days: It was an order book, a wish book, a source of good pictures, and toilet paper for the outhouses.

We always did our shopping at Myers' store, because Mr. Myers was so nice and our friend Mr. Simmons had part ownership in it. Rudisill's was the biggest store, but we were loyal to Mr. Myers and Mr. Simmons. Also, Fireballs, the only other grocery store, sold liquor, so we couldn't shop there.

Both Myers and Fireballs were very narrow, dark stores with pot belly stoves. The groceries were on shelves behind the counter, and they went clear to the ceiling.

Anne Dwier, who was Mr. Myers' clerk, would usually be the one to take my list and pick the food cans or bread from the shelves behind her. If the items were on a high shelf she would run a ladder along the track to the desired location and climb up to get them. I was fascinated by Anne because of the way she could pop chewing gum. I never heard anyone who could pop it so loudly and so rhythmically.

Mr. Myers sold many other things besides groceries: coats, shoes, garden tools, and seeds.

One day Mama asked me to run to the store and get sandwich bread. When I told Anne, she handed me a jar of mayonnaise-looking stuff. She said, "Here's your sandwich spread."

I was startled at this new interpretation of what I thought I was supposed to get. But then, after saying it a few times, I decided that must have been what Mama meant. It's a good thing Anne knew, I thought.

(I never paid for the things I bought. Anne or Mr. Myers wrote it down in their spiral notebook.)

I hurried home with my purchase, handing it to Mama with pleasure, thinking she would be pleased that I had understood and bought the right thing. My pleasure shriveled promptly though when she said, "What is this? I wanted bread, not spread. Patty, why did you buy this? We never use sandwich spread."

Chagrined, I had to return to the store and admit my mistake and make Anne feel bad, too.

Behind Myers' Store was the shoe repair shop. Lewis Johnson, the only black man I knew, repaired shoes. He was the only shoe repair man, so he had lots of business. I thought his shop smelled good—leather and shoe polish smells.

Simmons Garage was always a busy place. Mr. Simmons was there, with teasing words for me. His dad, old Mr. Simmons, was often there, too, sitting in the small office or standing over the mechanics, watching.

Mr. Simmons' two sons, Billy and Frank, helped him in the garage, when they weren't in school, as did Carroll (Fatty) Reid.

Shortly after we arrived in Eagle Rock, Billy joined the Army and Frank joined the Navy, and both went off to war. They, along with many other Eagle Rock boys, became blue stars on a banner hanging in the back of our church.

When two soldiers from our congregation were killed, their stars were changed into gold. The stars gave a mystical quality to the soldiers and sailors, all of whom were heroes in my eyes.

Daddy made them even more special and different from everybody else by entering their names onto a typed list, which became dog-eared from much handling. He kept the list in his Bible and would bring it down each morning to the breakfast table. Sister and I would take turns reading the names of several boys from that list and two or three names from a missionary list for us to pray for. We would also read a verse of scripture.

One morning Daddy said, "Patsy Lake, you were not listening! What did I just say?"

My heart stood still as I listened to the words still vibrating in the air. I had not been listening to what he was saying, but now that he asked, I could still hear the words ringing in my ears. I quickly retrieved them and told him the exact words. He was satisfied, and I was grateful.

Our Grandpa Pylant in Purvis sent Sister and me each a $25 savings bond. I helped the war effort myself by buying a ten-cent U. S. Savings stamp each week. When I had bought enough stamps to purchase a $25 War Bond, I began saving my money in an account at the only bank in town. My savings account grew only slowly, however, because I couldn't resist buying books. Perhaps it was good that the book-buying trips to Roanoke were rare. By the time we left Eagle Rock, I had almost sixty dollars in my account.

I often picked up the mail at the Post Office. We didn't have a box. I just walked up to the window and asked the Postmaster for our mail. Sometimes in the spring I would hear a lot of "peep peeps" coming from behind the postmaster. Big boxes with holes in them and little yellow heads peaking out were coming in to the families who had ordered them from catalogs. Oh, how I wished for one of those boxes! I also worried that people might not pick them up before the chicks got hungry.

Mail was very important in those days, because people kept in touch with their family and friends through letters. No one in Eagle Rock ever called long distance unless it was a great emergency. When that happened, one had to go to Central's office to make the call. The whole family would go along and stand quietly while Central tried to make the connection. When she finally got the requested party on the line, everyone listened while the daddy shouted into the telephone.

5
The Church

It was in Eagle Rock that I first fell in love with Jesus. I really listened to most of Daddy's sermons, and I believed every word he said. The collective impact of those sermons, frequent talks with Daddy, Sunday School, Vacation Bible School, Gama, and our breakfast devotionals led me into knowing that I loved Jesus very much. He was part of the fabric of my life. Mother, Daddy, Gama, Aunt Yuba, and Miss Lucy were very good representatives of Jesus. I knew him, believed in him, and committed my life to him as far as I knew how as a seven year old.

One Sunday afternoon during the first summer we were in Eagle Rock, our church had a baptizing in Craig's Creek. There were a lot of people to be baptized, many of them kids. New Christians had been waiting all through the winter for this occasion. It was a bright, hot day, and I was excited about the whole affair. I took Daddy aside and asked him if I could be baptized.

He asked me, "Do you believe that Jesus is God's Son sent to save us?"

"Oh, Daddy, you know I do."

Daddy continued, wanting to be sure it wasn't just the hot day and the thought of getting into the water that was motivating my sudden request, "Have you asked Jesus to save you and come and live in you?"

"Yes."

"And you want to live for him the rest of your life?"

I couldn't believe Daddy had to ask me these questions. Of course, I wanted to live for Jesus. I had believed Daddy's sermons. I had told Jesus how much I loved him many times.

Satisfied that I understood all I was capable of understanding at that age and that I had committed all I knew how to commit, Daddy said, "Okay, Patsy Lake. Line up with the others."

I was so excited I could hardly contain myself. Daddy presented me to the church gathered on the bank, and they voted me in. Daddy then took the candidates for baptism aside and went through his baptizing instructions with them. The rest of our church stood on the bank watching. We took off our shoes and stepped into the creek.

I had on a feed sack dress with a strip of organdy sewed across the top to make it a Sunday dress.

As each person's turn came, he waded over to Daddy. Daddy always said, "I baptize you

now, my sister (or my brother), in the name of the Father, and of the Son, and of the Holy Ghost." And with that he would place the folded handkerchief the candidate had brought for that purpose over the candidate's face and lower him into the water.

When he got to me, I noticed he changed the wording to "my daughter." I suppose it would have been hard for him to call me "my sister." In this commitment to Jesus, I think I really was his new sister, but it made me feel special and unique that I was called something different from everyone else.

As I sat in our Sunday evening service the next Sunday, I wondered if I really had trusted Jesus in the right way, or if I had just wanted to get into the creek. Afraid I hadn't done it right, tears rolled down my cheeks, and I said from the bottom of my heart, "I love you, I love you, Jesus. I want to be with you forever."

After that I knew I was a member of the Church, for sure. If I had not been fervent enough at Craig's Creek, I was now. The week after that, when we had the Lord's Supper, I very respect fully took a piece of the bread that was passed around, and the little glass of grape juice.

Mama told Daddy he was getting better and better with his sermons. At first he had to look at his notes a lot, but now he only glanced down from time to time, and he could put more expression into what he was saying.

My favorite sermons were the ones where he sang at the end. He had the best voice I had ever heard, and I took the words of the songs very seriously.

I especially liked the sermon where he used the story "Pippa Passes," by Robert Browning. He would conclude by singing one of his all-time favorite songs.

> You may have the joybells a-ringing in
> your heart. . .

In fact, this was the song he woke Sister and me up with every morning. I didn't like it so much in the early morning, but in church I listened and learned.

Daddy didn't laugh much, but he smiled and was happy deep down so he sang joy songs and taught me a joy verse. My first Bible verse, which I learned when I was about 4 years old, was "A merry heart is a good medicine." Proverbs 17:22.

After I was baptized, I began to memorize scripture in earnest: Psalm 23, Psalm 100, John 3:16, Romans 3:23, Romans 6:23, the Christmas story in Luke, and many others.

Someone had given me a Bible card game that had the name of one book of the Bible on each card, with questions about it for playing the game. I liked to play the game with my friends, because I had memorized all the answers and was always the winner. I also used these cards for memorizing the books of the Bible. I would memorize as far as I could pronounce the names. When I came to a hard one, I would run ask Mama how to say it. Names like Nahum, Habakkuk, Zephaniah, Haggai, Zechariah, and Malachi I had not heard before.

After I learned the names of all the books, I would practice finding them in my zipper Bible. I got to be so fast, I beat everyone else in looking up scriptures at our Wednesday night prayer meetings. Mr. Simmons said, "We might as well quit. Patsy Lake is going to get there first."

Because Mama thought I was so good at looking up scripture, she wrote off for the rules to the Bible Drill contest that would be held at the Massanetta Baptist Assembly the next summer. I memorized the verses and drilled and drilled, but when time for the contest arrived, I was afraid and begged Mama not to make me do it. She said okay and let me out of it. Later, I was so sorry that I didn't do it, I cried.

Massanetta was another wonder of my Eagle Rock days. Our church rented a cabin for the week, so we could all stay together. Mama made up a silly song to get everyone interested in going.

> I'm going to wake up in the morning at
>   Massanetta Springs—yippee!
> Where the Baptists come a-trottin' from
>   the land of cotton
> And everything's heavenly!
> I'm gonna find out all I can about these
>   Baptists—yes siree!
> These cunning, stunning gals and
>   lads......
> O Mama pin a rose on me. (Stamp stamp)

The first thing we kids did when our bus pulled into Massanetta Springs was to race to the spring house behind the big hotel. We would hang our heads over the side and look down into the water. Some people had thrown pennies into it, and that was hard to believe. We sure didn't. Every five pennies was a nickel, and that was an ice cream cone.

I attended classes part of the time we were there and went to worship services until I met a little girl named Janice. She never wanted to go. Instead, she wanted me to play with her, so I often stayed away from the services and did. Mama and Daddy probably thought I was too young to get much out of the services or thought maybe they were too long for me, or something. But I got tired of staying with Janice and missing out on what everyone else was doing. I tried to get her to go with me. But she wouldn't, and Mama kept "letting" me stay with her. That summer I felt as if I had wasted the week. I was glad Janice did not come the next year, and I was able to go to everything with our group.

The first summer we went to Massanetta, I did a musical reading, "Me and my Brother Jimmy," for the talent show, with Mama playing the piano background. I won first place! Everywhere we went after that, people wanted me to do "Me and my Brother Jimmy."

Me and my brother Jimmy, we go to bed at night,
With all the windows fastened and all the doors shut tight.
It gets a little stuffy, but neither of us cares.
We hear the awfulest noises when we haven't said our prayers.

When the winds a-blowing—oh, goodness, gracious me!
You never can imagine what me and Jimmy hears.
Those slippery, sliding footsteps come creeping up the stairs,
And prowl around the landing, when we haven't said our prayers.

Shimmery, shaky shadows creep across the wall,
And stand beside our bedpost before heading for the hall.
The moon shines through the windows and stares and stares and STARES.
Just like a ghost or something, when we haven't said our prayers.

Last night as we were lying, a-shivering in bed,
I pulled all the covers up around my head.
I grabbed ahold of Jimmy and kind of squeezed his hand,
—and said, "Tomorrow, we'll pray to beat the band!" [3]

---

[3] Source unknown.

I don't think it would have been very good without the piano. The piano made the sounds of the wind blowing, and the slippery footsteps coming up the stairs, till it scared me to say it.

The next year Sister and I sang a song together and were asked to sing it on the radio program in nearby Harrisonburg: "No Longer Sleeping in Mossy Dale."

> All earth today is bright and gay, with
>   sunshine and with song
> With blossoms sweet, the flowers greet
>   and join the happy throng.
> No longer sleeping in Mossy Dale, the
>   flowers awake with the day,
> Their heads uplifted to greet the sun, they
>   praise the Lord alway.
> His loving kindness, his tender care is o'er
>   the great and the small.
> He lives bestowing on all below Him,
>   blessings unto us all.[4]

Sister sang the melody and I sang alto. I did not really know what alto was, but it was what I always sang. When our family stood around the piano to sing at home, I always sat on the piano bench next to Mama, and she sang

---

[4] Source unknown.

a strong alto so close to my ears, it became the melody to me.

By the next summer when we went to Massanetta, I was playing a cornet and Sister was playing a trombone. Naturally, that was our talent show act—a horn duet. We played "My Mother's Bible." It almost went too high for me, but we won second place. We got to play that on the radio, and Daddy sang on the radio, too.

Another wonderful thing our church did was to have a two-week long Vacation Bible School every summer. Every weekday morning for two whole weeks! It was a highlight of the summer, like Massanetta.

Daddy was the Vacation Bible School principal. We kids would line up in two lines by age group in front of the church. Three older kids would be selected each day to carry the American flag, the Christian flag, and the Bible. Mama would begin to play a stately march on the piano and we would begin to march up the stairs

into the building and down the aisle to fill up the front four or five pews on each side.

Daddy taught us a ritual of mottoes, scriptures, and songs that we went through every morning. At the end of our reciting and singing, the Beginners (ages 4 and 5) went to their room to begin their activities. The rest of us stayed for a story: a missionary story one day and a character story the next.

When we went to our separate rooms, the wonders continued. There were activities with scripture, and flannel board stories, and songs. We began to put together a notebook of verses and pictures.

Then there was refreshment time, for which everyone had brought his own cup.

Then several of the age groups came together for handwork. It was so much fun, I could hardly bear for it to end.

One year Gama was staying with us at Vacation Bible School time, and she taught my class. Everyone loved her, and I was so proud of her! She had such unusual stories and things to do. She taught us the disciple song to the tune of "Jesus Loves Me."

> Jesus called them one by one, Peter,
>   Andrew, James, and John,
> Next came Philip, Thomas too, Matthew
>   and Bartholomew.
> James the one they called the Less; Simon,
>   also, Thaddeus.
> The twelfth apostle Judas made; Jesus was
>   by him betrayed.

While we sang the song, one of us kids put the disciples on the flannel board. We all wanted to do that, and we waved our hands in the air, hoping to be chosen.

Gama had a big cardboard fold-out book that unfolded halfway across the room. We got to take turns unfolding the book. On each page, as it unfolded, she had pasted pictures to illustrate the song we sang.

The Bible is the best book, the Book we
   hold so dear,
A story book, a picture book, a book of
   songs to cheer,
The Bible tells of Jesus, who's in his home
   above.
The Bible tells the message sweet, that God
   is Love.

Gama had three rolls of narrow red, white, and black ribbons sewed together, that she used to tell us the story of salvation. Each roll would begin with white to show the innocence of a new baby. But soon we came to black, when the child got old enough to know right from wrong, and chose to do wrong. Then the child heard the story of Jesus at Sunday School— (here we came to the red ribbon). Then back to black, and back to red, until the first child accepted Jesus at a young age.

That ribbon became white for the rest of its length.

The second ribbon continued alternating black and red until almost the end of life. A conversion at an old age brought us to white ribbon, but there wasn't much time left to serve the Lord.

The third ribbon alternated black and red until it ran out, still on black. Gama had a real good story line that went with each ribbon, describing the life that accepted Jesus early; the life that kept putting it off but finally came to him in old age; and the life that put off the decision to follow Jesus too long.

Then she had two ribbons that were sewed together in circles. One was a white circle, representing being in Heaven forever and ever. The other was a black circle, representing Hell forever and ever.

On the last day of Bible School we practiced for our Commencement. Returning that evening we performed for all the parents. All the kids dressed up in their best clothes, marched in to the music, saluted the flags and the Bible, said and sang our ritual of verses and songs. Then each class marched to the platform, one class at a time, performing something it had learned during the week.

After our program was over, we proudly took our parents to our classrooms to see the notebooks and handcrafts we had made.

We got to take everything home afterward, which seemed so great at the time. But the next day, looking at all my creations at home alone, there was not nearly the same spark to them, and I longed for the school to continue.

Mama, the woman who would someday start the Church Recreation Service of the Southern Baptist Convention, led in all kinds of celebrations at Daddy's three little churches. As I look back, I wonder how she could always have been so full of energy, sparkle, and creativity. I think she *looked* ordinary enough, being 5 feet 2 inches tall with dark brown hair.

But there was a charisma about her that electrified her audiences and ignited enthusiasm. People responded to her with an eagerness to be part of the fun or whatever plan her fertile brain was concocting. She could make very plain, simple things important, maybe because she cared so much and loved people. She built people up and brought out the best in them.

At Christmastime there was always a pageant. I remember one year when we did "Christmas Eve in a Christian Home." She wove into that pageant all the talent each little church could yield. The kids in the "family" on the stage would gather around the mother and father to have a Christmas program. One kid would play the piano, one would sing a song, and the mother and father would perform in some way. Then they heard carolers singing outside (off-stage). After listening to the carolers, the family invited them in to sing more songs with everyone gathered around the piano. Then they all sat down on the floor and listened to Father read the Christmas story. Just as he finished reading, we heard sleigh bells.

The front door to the sanctuary where we were gathered blew open and there was Santa Claus with his big pack on his back. He struggled down the aisle with his heavy load, wishing us a merry Christmas with a lot of "ho ho's." The kids were completely awestruck. I know I was. He opened his bag and gave gifts to all the kids.

Mother's parties and banquets were well-planned, prepared, and exciting! I guess they should be. She wrote plans for parties and banquets that were regularly published in *The Baptist Training Union Magazine*, and someday she would write the best party and banquet books ever. No big city church had finer banquets or more fun parties than our church had.

Of course, our banquets and parties were all-church affairs. I felt as much a part of them as anyone else. The basement of the Eagle Rock church would be completely transformed for the banquets—with decorations hanging from the ceiling, table decorations, favors at each plate, and everyone dressed in his finest. Many wore homemade, long dresses. I don't know how Mother came up with such fine programs, but she did. She would work with people and train them to do stunts, sing duets, and recite poems—people who had never done such things.

Our Halloween party one year ended up in the graveyard. Someone told a story about an awful wreck and how the body parts were

scraped up off the pavement. In the darkness we passed the "parts" around and were supposed to guess what part it was. (Grapes were the eyes, a piece of cow's liver was the brain, ropes of spaghetti were the intestines. There was hair—that was someone's hairpiece.) It all scared me to death.

Another special church occasion that took place in the cemetery was our Easter sunrise service. Since the cemetery was on a high hill overlooking the town, it was a perfect spot to gather in the early morning grayness and watch the sun come up, while we sang and read the scripture about Jesus' rising from the dead.

Then, of course, there were funerals that ended in the cemetery. The cemetery was divided into sections according to denomination. The biggest, prettiest section was the Methodist one. That's where the whole town gathered when Mr. Myers died. The Baptist section was fenced off and was not nearly as well kept.

The funerals I attended made a deep impression on me, for they were my first experiences with death. They scared me quite a bit, especially two that were for kids: one of my classmates, Jo Ann Van Ness, who drowned in the James River; and Hubert Biggs, Sister's age, who was hit in the head by a baseball when he

bent over to put sand on his hands before batting. Another sad funeral was that of a young mother in our congregation, Louise Honts.

As I saw their caskets being lowered into the ground, it was hard for me to grasp that they were still alive, but with Jesus now. I wish my parents had spent more time helping me see that reality. Maybe they did the best they could. Maybe they thought I understood. What seemed to take center stage in my mind were the horrible tales of how my friends died. Now they were gone. Death in a small town could not be hidden from kids. We all shared in it.

When revival meetings came to our town, everyone turned out for them—every night. The church would be packed. It was a big event.

The guest preacher would stay with us in our beautiful guest room. It was the one really pretty room in our house. Louise and Ed Honts donated the bed for the room, and the rose colored linoleum. Daddy made a dresser for it, using two apple crates with a board across the top. He covered the top with wallpaper under plate glass. Mama made a blue skirt to go around it, using blue cotton for the underskirt, covered with blue net. The seat for the dresser was a small barrel with a matching skirt and cushioned top. It may not sound pretty, but it was.

The revival preacher and Daddy visited the people in town during the day and drove up into the mountains looking for more to invite. For exercise and a "fun" activity, Daddy would let the revival preacher take a few runs at mowing the grass on our hill with the push lawnmower. This was very good exercise, since there were no gas motor lawnmowers then.

Once a reformed alcoholic spoke at our church. His life made for such a terrible story, but it ended with a powerful and dramatic conversion experience. I thought about it, and I told Daddy, "I will never be a witness like that, because I will never be an alcoholic. My life is so ordinary. What will I ever be able to say for Jesus?"

Daddy said, "You will have a testimony about the power of Jesus to keep you clean and pure, instead of a converted alcoholic's testimony. Your testimony will be far better, because it will show the good that comes from obeying Jesus all your life. I would rather have that testimony by far." That was a thought I pondered long and hard. It was hard for an eight-year-old to see how that could be so, but I hoped it was.

When there was no one else around to go visiting with Daddy, I sometimes went with him. We discovered families living way back in the mountains by themselves.

There was one family that lived in a house with dirt floors, with animals coming and going freely. The little girls were named: Ruby, Jewel, and Pearl. Their looks did not match their names, for they were very dirty.

We took Jewel home with us for a week during Vacation Bible School. She was my age and didn't know how to use knives and forks. And she didn't know about taking baths. But she was very quiet and did everything she was told to do.

6
Our Animals

One of the first things Daddy did on our arrival in Eagle Rock was to transform the coal house in the backyard into a goat house. He partitioned a small section off to store hay and feed. The larger section was for our new goat, Annabelle. Annabelle was a white, Saanen goat. I did not particularly like her milk. I thought it tasted "goaty."

Daddy said, "Saanens usually have the best milk, but Annabelle's milk does have a rather distinctive flavor. I wish we still had old Chico. Now she really gave good milk!"

I had often heard the story of Chico, the goat my folks had when Sister was a baby. She was a Toggenburg. Mama and Daddy had bought Chico because goat milk was the only milk Sister's stomach could digest. When they moved from Ft. Worth, Texas, at the end of Daddy's seminary training, to St. Petersburg, Florida, for his first job, they took the back seat out of their little Austen car and stowed Chico there. They swung a hammock for the baby at Chico's head. When the baby was hungry, they stopped and milked the goat. The milk was all warmed and ready to go!

But we were stuck with Annabelle, so we finally adjusted to the taste of her milk. Everybody else in town drank cows' milk. And it did not come in bottles as it had in Austin, where the milkman had delivered fresh pasteurized milk to our front doorstep every morning. Here, if you did not have your own cow, you bought raw milk that the farmers brought to town and took it home in a jar.

We didn't have a goat during the first five years of my life, but as soon as it was possible, Daddy bought Annabelle. From then on, we always had a goat.

If we visited out of town for a week or more, Daddy would rent a goat. He would not just buy milk. He would pay some farmer to let him milk one of his goats once a day.

Daddy was very particular about the milking. He petted and talked lovingly to his rented goat. He sang softly to her as he washed and dried her udder before he started milking. He said if the goat was scared or uptight, she would hold up her milk. He continued to talk to her, pausing to massage her udder from time to time, coaxing her to let down the milk. He milked into a clean pan with a handle, and then he would strain the milk through a clean cloth into a jar and refrigerate it as soon as possible.

When drinking raw milk, I guess it's important to be picky. And, of course, it always makes sense to be kind and loving—especially if you want cooperation.

Our first cat, Sam, didn't live much past early adulthood. Just as I was getting very attached to him, he got sick and lay by the stove, day after day. Mama pushed big capsules down his throat.

One day Sam was very stiff, and Mama said he was dead. Then I really cried. Daddy tried to console me by offering to have a funeral for him. All the kids in the neighborhood came and watched as we lowered Sam into his grave on the little rug he had died on. We marked his grave in our backyard with stones, and for a long time I made regular visits to it.

Soon my pain was relieved by the arrival of Sam II. Sam II looked just like the first Sam. He was black and white and grew to be huge. My folks acquired him to get rid of our mouse population. He was an excellent mouser and found plenty to occupy his time—and feed his appetite—in our big, barny house.

We had a small handbell that had been given to me when we left our Austin church. My Sunday School teacher let me pick my gift and sometimes I was sorry I had picked the bell. Everyone in the neighborhood knew it was time for the Pylant girls to come home when the bell rang. That bell interrupted many a good game and was never a welcome sound. If Sam was out cruising the neighborhood, he would come home, too, when the bell rang.

Sadly, I would have to give up this Sam, too, when we moved in 1945. I don't think he was sad, though. The Reynolds, across the road from us, had been loving him for a long time, and he had been taking care of their mice, too. So it was a natural transition for him. His heart was not nearly as heavy as mine at our separation. When we returned for a visit a year later, he was fatter than ever and almost too lazy for the mouse business.

My own personal pet was a small turtle named Hercules. It was fascinating to watch his cute little head, with its green stripes and red markings. A U.S. flag was painted on his shell.

I would hold him up by the shell and look at his yellow bottom side and watch his legs work. I put a rock in his dish so he could climb out of the shallow water. His food consisted of smelly, dried bugs that we bought. He pulled his head into his shell to sleep.

As winter approached, I became alarmed that Hercules always had his head tucked into his shell and didn't eat the food I gave him. Later, someone told me he was hybernating and would sleep until spring. I continued to change his water and sprinkle in a little food occasionally just in case he woke up.

When warm and then hot summer came, I fixed a pen for Hercules outside, sinking his dish into the ground in the center of the pen and keeping water in it.

This was not a good move for Hercules. He did not get nearly as much attention outside. I often forgot to look at him for days. And then one day when I did look, I discovered someone had smashed Hercules with a rock and broken his dish. One of our small neighborhood boys admitted doing it. I cried a little, but was soon pacified by the interesting job of making Hercules a casket and burying him.

7
Camping

"Help, Daddy, help!" I waved my arms and shielded my face from the fierce attackers that seemed to have appeared from nowhere. A black cloud of angry hornets had swarmed from their nest to avenge my trespassing. I was too dazed to run, but Daddy moved quickly, dragging me into the creek a few feet away.

For many years I associated camping with hornets. And it had started out to be such a wonderful treat! The Thomases, who belonged to Longdale Church, invited us to stay in a cabin by the creek on their farm. Mama didn't come. I suppose it was a little too rustic for her. Or could it be that her idea of the perfect vacation was a quiet, empty house?

The cabin was devoid of furniture of any kind, but we brought blankets to lie on. Someone loaned Daddy a fold-up army cot. There was the usual outhouse with its old torn-up Sears-Roebuck catalog.

As soon as we arrived, we dumped our belongings in the cabin and made a dash for the creek. Swimming pools were non-existent in Eagle Rock, so we didn't want to waste a minute of this extra-special opportunity.

I cannot say that I swam, because I didn't know how. I just had fun playing in the water until Daddy scared me by holding me up in the water and telling me to kick my legs and paddle my arms. I was so afraid he would turn me loose that, of course, I did no good.

We should have stayed in the water the rest of the day, as it turned out. But without foreknowledge, we happily splashed out after awhile to take a stroll. After all, we would have lots of swimming time.

That stroll along the shore of the creek with the Thomas girls was perhaps the most memorable and awful time of my life up to that point.

Sister and Frankie Thomas walked just ahead of Daddy and me. Their path led them under a low-hanging branch, which they pushed out of their way. It snapped back and forth when they released it.

Just as Daddy and I got there, hornets swarmed out. "Has our home been damaged? Who did it?" they seemed to buzz.

They seized on me as the likely culprit and settled down on my unsuspecting form like a black cloud, stinging and stinging. Fire shot through my arms, my legs, my face, my whole body! I screamed as Daddy beat them off me, dragging me into the creek. The pain and burning was fierce! The attack was so sudden, I had no idea what was happening.

Daddy was stung, too, but I had more exposed flesh in my shorts, bolero top and bare feet.

Daddy and the girls took me to the Thomas farmhouse and put various remedies on me. However, they had no magic potion, and the pain continued unabated.

As I sat on their screened porch in the evening, my ears pounded and burned and swelled. I watched my ears grow in the shadow on the wall. The fact that the others had gone on about their carefree play escaped my notice. Just breathing took all my energy. One eye swelled completely shut and other parts of my body swelled and throbbed and burned. I wanted to go home so badly, thinking surely Mama could make the pain stop.

But we did not go home. We went out to our cabin by the creek to spend the night. It was a miserable night. I could not find a comfortable position to sleep in on that hard floor, so Daddy gave me his cot. That wasn't much better. My ears were too huge to lie on and my arms and sides hurt.

Morning finally came, and we cut our trip

short, packed up and went home. Mama would be surprised to see us coming home so soon, I thought. I could hardly wait to tell her what had happened and get her sympathy.

She *was* properly shocked and pained over my experience. "Patty, what happened? You must be allergic to bees! Oh, I know it hurts."

But even Mama could not make me well. That would take time.

Gradually, gradually, the fires began to cool and the swelling went down. In the meantime, I made the circuit of my friends, showing off my wounds—expecting and getting lots of good attention.

8
Health Remedies

"Cut out the sweets and meats, Patsy Lake." I had just mentioned that I had a sore throat. Now a deeper dread settled over me.

Daddy had several distasteful remedies for sickness, so we certainly never faked being sick. The first step when sickness hit (a sore throat, mouth ulcer, cold, etc.) was to "cut out the sweets and meats." There wasn't much to cut out, except Gama's wonderful homemade guava marmalade and jelly from Florida. I did love that on my whole wheat biscuits. And as I have already explained, meat did not often appear on our table. However, now it was total abstinence.

The next inevitable horror was Citrocarbonate. It was a cure for all ills. Daddy mixed the powder in a glass of water and tried to get us interested by letting us watch the fizzing. That never worked after the first time. It was bad. And we were expected to drink the whole glass. I tried holding my breath and swallowing as fast as I could, but there was a lot in that glass.

Then Daddy thought of a wonderful embellishment to Citrocarbonate. He mixed it in orange juice (canned orange juice). He talked this up as a wonderful soda. "This is really good," he would say as he smacked his lips. "Hmm-mm, you'll love this."

Frothy on top, it did look good. But the first disappointing taste turned into a gagging experience, clear to the bottom. I really hated to get sick.

If we had a fever, Mama and Daddy would pile covers on us to make us sweat. But we didn't sweat; the fever just climbed higher. I would have terrible nightmares of grotesque shapes moving around me. I would visualize water dripping from a faucet, or the water fountain at school, or water running from any source I had ever seen. But they would only let me have enough water to wet my lips. No food and no water. Fortunately, my fever always broke before going too high, and the welcome sweat soaked me.

I had many upset stomach episodes in those days, when I could keep nothing down. This would continue until I could think of some food I really, really wanted. As soon as I named it, Mama would turn the world upside down to find it, because that would always be the food that would settle my stomach. One time it was pineapple, and she was able to find a can of pineapple at Myers. It did the trick.

The hard one came when I wanted jello, very badly. After each convulsion of vomiting passed and I was at peace for a little while, I would plead, "Please, Mama, please. I want jello. Red jello."

Because of the war, jello was not available in Eagle Rock. But the word got around town that Patsy Lake needed jello. When Mrs. Burkholder, who lived at the end of Main Street, just west of the Post Office, heard about Mama's desperate search, she called to say that she had some. Wonderful, beautiful red jello, and my stomach settled. I hardly knew Mrs. Burkholder and wondered how she could give away her jello—to me, a near stranger. I often thought of her later, when I found it hard to give away something I liked and wanted to keep for myself.

Preventive medicine was a big deal in our household. At first we had tasty chewable vitamins at the breakfast table every morning. But when Daddy thought we were old enough to swallow capsules, our vitamins progressed to the mail-order "pearls" that he took.

He was careful about our diet, making sure we ate a variety of vegetables. Bananas and citrus fruit were not available, except canned orange juice. He was evidently able to get hold of an occasional lemon, because we sometimes had lemon water for an after-school treat. (That's lemonade without sugar.)

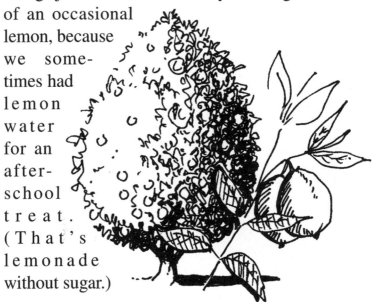

He went to the mill and bought whole wheat kernels. These he would cook until they popped open. This would be his cereal. And ours when he didn't give us a choice.

If we had a choice, Sister would have oatmeal, and I would have Wheaties. I loved Wheaties. I wanted them every morning. Mama had bacon (when she could get it), eggs, and coffee. She controlled her own regimen.

Wheaties was the breakfast of champions, and I once ordered a few of their "champion pamphlets." I ordered pamphlets on how to be a swimming champion and how to be a bowling champion. (No matter that I never got to go swimming, except once or twice in the summer in the creek; and I had never seen a bowling alley.) I was very disappointed when the pamphlets didn't help me to become a champion in either field.

One summer there was an outbreak of polio in town. Or at least Jackie Fridley, who lived just up the hill from us, got it. We were all very scared of it, especially since the folks in town talked of nothing else. There was much respect for the word "quarantine". Jackie came through okay, so it must not have been a very bad case.

9
Chores

I didn't have many jobs when Aunt Yuba was not with us. But there were some. I have already mentioned that it was Sister's and my job to bring in the wood. At ages six and eight we were not very strong or efficient, so Daddy ended up carrying most of it.

We never made up our beds in the winter. We just jumped out of bed and ran to the stove in the kitchen.

We helped with the garden, pulling weeds and picking bugs off the squash. There again we were not much help, I'm sure. We helped pick blackberries, but the thorns were so bad and I was so slow and careful, my bowl didn't fill up very fast.

I began ironing the handkerchiefs and napkins when I was 7 or 8. Mama sprinkled them down with water and wadded them up in a basket.

She set up the ironing board near the telephone. I heard her bragging on me to someone on the telephone, telling them what a perfect job I did on them. I proudly smoothed out the next napkin, ironed it, folded it, ironed again. After she hung up and came to pick up the stack of napkins, her expression of pleasure changed to surprise.

"Patty, these napkins are still wet! Maybe I bragged on you too soon."

She didn't mean to hurt my feelings, but all my pride drained away and I was suddenly ashamed. I promised myself that next time I would get them dry. And, of course, there was a next time.

We used cloth napkins at every meal, with a painted clothespin on each so we could know which was whose. Some of the napkins were made out of feedsacks, but Gama tried to make them fancy by sewing the edges in scallops.

One of the funniest jobs Daddy offered some of the neighborhood kids and me was to help him clear our hillside yard of rocks. We were to throw the rocks at the back of our (unpainted) garage. We thought he said that he would pay us a penny for each rock, so we threw with gusto, energized by the thought we were racking up the money.

However, after we had thrown rocks for hours (it seemed), we went to collect our pay and discovered that we had misunderstood. *He* said that he had told us he'd pay us a penny for every *ten* rocks. The mountains of wealth that had been accruing in our minds as we watched the rock pile grow suddenly melted away. So did the kids. I was left on my own to pick up rocks.

When the kids left, I let out some kind of mournful expletive, like "Gee Willikens."

Daddy heard me and said, "Don't say 'Gee,' Patsy Lake. It comes from 'Jesus' and you don't want to take the Lord's name in vain."

"Well, then, I'll say 'Golly'."

"No, don't say that either. It comes from 'God.' And so does 'Gosh', so don't say 'Gosh'."

"But Daddy, what can I say? Sometimes you have to say something when you hurt yourself."

"You can say, 'Ouch,' 'Ow,' or 'Oh.' That's enough to say."

I practiced saying "Oh" a few times. It wasn't very satisfying, and I didn't think it accomplished the same thing that the other words did. But I wanted to please Daddy, so I thought I'd try to stick with "Oh."

In the days that followed, I put together other combinations, like "Oh, dear." That was okay. "Oh, my goodness!" That was not okay. Only God is Goodness. Only God is Gracious. That knocked out two other possibilities. I came up with more imaginative expressions and tried them out on Daddy. "Holy Moly." (No good); "Clippety Clop!" "Wow!" "My word!," "Jeepers Creepers." They were okay, but Daddy didn't think they were necessary. "Why do you need to say anything?"

I don't remember ever hearing him use an expletive. I never saw him get excited or upset. He was quiet and calm and deliberate in all that he did.

Every Monday was wash day in Eagle Rock, wash day for everyone. When I came home from school for lunch on Mondays, washing machine and tubs filled the kitchen. The hot water stove would be roaring. The washing machine would swish the clothes in sudsy, very hot water. Rinso or Duz were the big detergents of the day, highly advertised on radio: "Rinso white, Rinso bright." "Duz does everything!" Mama used Rinso.

When Mama thought the clothes had washed long enough, she took a wooden spoon and lifted them piece by piece from the hot, sudsy water and fed them one by one through the wringer. It was fascinating to watch the flattened towels come through the wringer and plop into a tub of plain water. After they were all out of the washer, Mama moved the wringer to the front of the plain water tub, where the water was now looking a bit sudsy. She would pick the clothes up with her hands from this tub and feed them through the wringer again. They would plop into the next tub of plain water.

It looked like a lot of fun, and I wanted to feed the clothes through the wringer. After all the warnings about not getting my fingers caught in the wringer and hearing the horror tales of those who did, I wasn't quite as eager. But still, it was kind of fun, as long as I could stop the "game" when I had had enough.

I was more useful to Mama at the clothesline. I stood by her and handed her the clothes, one at a time, so she didn't have to bend over.

Obviously, Mama and Daddy had many, many jobs,

but for the most part Sister and I were free to just be kids—to read and roam and play. Nothing organized, except for the few church activities.

As I crawled into bed each night, I felt safe, and loved, and that all was right with the world. I could not imagine it being any other way. So perhaps my prayer each night was routine. But I never failed to say a long extended thank you to God and ask His blessing on each individual friend and relative—aunt, uncle, and cousin—calling each by name. Since I would say this prayer out loud, it became a real nuisance to Sister, who finally said in exasperation, "For goodness sake, Patty! Lump 'em up."

Thank you, God, for the little town and the parents who made possible my golden age of childhood. Thank you for parents who believed in me and loved me unconditionally. I am forever grateful for the opportunity I had to live in a community where Your way was the accepted way of life! That surely helped build a solid base for the rest of my life. For the security, support, fun, acceptance, and love I experienced in Eagle Rock I will always give you thanks.

I love you.

Patsy Lake

Epilogue

In 1945 my family moved from Eagle Rock to Oak Hill Baptist Academy at Mouth of Wilson, Virginia. We lived in the boys' dormitory in four rooms that were partitioned off for us at one end of the first floor. We ate many of our meals in the dining hall.

In 1945 Oak Hill was very "rural." There was no indoor plumbing when we arrived, but Daddy soon installed a bathroom and kitchen sink for us. The nearest telephone was thirteen miles away at Independence. Mama made an appeal to Virginia Baptists for washing machines for the school. The Baptist Board not only came up with several new Bendix washing machines for the use of the students, but had them installed.

In addition to their many other jobs, Daddy taught Bible and Mama taught piano. No one in town actually had a piano. The first time Mama sat down to play ours, she was startled to discover that she had an immediate and large audience. As soon as the first note sounded, students clustered at the open windows, jostling for position. Because of the intense interest, Mama offered to teach piano to any students able to find a piano on which to practice. Not only did pianos appear in the homes, but one also appeared in the auditorium, located on the second floor of the school building. The little unpainted houses that were clumped near the textile mill in Mouth of Wilson were soon reverberating with the sound of music.

The school was small. Many students lived

on the campus, but many came from the surrounding hills, brought in by buses. The first, second, and third grades were in one room. I was a fifth grader at the time we arrived, and the fifth grade shared a room with the fourth grade. The sixth and seventh grades were together. The high school classes met in the two or three remaining rooms. Sister went away to school, becoming a boarding student at Montreat High School and College in Montreat, N.C. Though our family income was less than it had been at Eagle Rock, we did not have many expenses.

In 1947 Dr. Bill Marshall, who had just become the new president of Wayland Baptist College in Plainview, Texas, stopped by to ask Mama and Daddy to join the faculty of the college. Daddy (Lake R. Pylant) would be Dean of Men and teach classes in Bible and Religious Education. Mama (Agnes Durant Pylant) would be Dean of Women and teach Speech and Drama. They accepted, and we moved to the barren plains of West Texas. After the plush mountains and flowing streams and rivers of Virginia, West Texas was a shock. Again, we lived in the boys' dormitory, a new building called McDonald Hall.

My life changed radically. Plainview was a big city to me, with 14,000 residents according to the city limits signs. The transition was made so much harder for me, because in the transition I skipped two grades. I certainly had not intended to do such a thing. Mr. Ussery, our Oak Hill principal, with all good intentions, coached me through a seventh grade math book before we left so I could go into the eighth grade. By so doing, I could still graduate at the same time my Oak Hill friends did in Virginia's eleven-year system. Eighth grade would have been a good thing. But the eighth grade in Virginia is the first year of high school. I suppose it was a natural next step for Daddy to think that since I had been promoted to high school in Virginia, I should be in high school in Texas. Oh, how I wished Daddy had just let me go into the eighth grade with kids closer to my age. That was already skipping one year. But he went to school with me on registration day and signed me up to be a freshman in Plainview High School, the ninth grade. Ninth grade kids were very grown-up. I was still a little girl—twelve years old. I still had pigtails. I rode my newly acquired bicycle to school, though I didn't do that for many mornings. Girls did not ride bicycles to high school, I discovered. So I walked the fourteen blocks from our apartment in

McDonald Hall, carrying my heavy books.

The first two years were social disasters, though I did well enough academically. By my junior year I was beginning to catch up physically, and by my senior year I felt accepted. I was the salutatorian of the class and eager to attend Wayland after graduation.

It was no wonder I wanted to attend Wayland. Mama and Daddy talked about it all the time. Sister was enrolled there and living in the girls' dormitory, Pioneer Hall. I attended all the basketball games with my folks. And of course, I wouldn't have missed one of Mama's plays. The Wayland auditorium was always packed with townspeople as well as students, because her plays were the best entertainment in town.

Sister graduated from Wayland and got married. I learned to fly airplanes and got my pilot's license on my 17th birthday. I worked at the airport on Saturdays and wrote "Plane Talk" for the *Plainview Herald*. At Wayland Mama started the first Church Recreation Department in the Southern Baptist Convention and also created a Speech Choir. After Daddy bought the family a four-seat Stinson airplane, he decided to learn to fly. He was caught in a major dust storm on his first solo cross-country flight, and his plane crashed in Amarillo in 1953. Daddy was dead at age 51.

I met Jimmie Monhollon in Mama's "Wayland Words" Speech Choir. We were married at the end of our junior year. After graduating from Wayland, we attended the University of Wyoming in Laramie and Vanderbilt University in Nashville.

I became a librarian, following the dream of my childhood. I interrupted that career very soon to be the mother of four children who were born in rapid succession—Mike, Melody, Marsha, and John. I felt totally fulfilled and happy as a full-time mother, Sunday School teacher, and church librarian. I remember saying that I must be in heaven already, because surely I could not be any happier. After my children left home for college, I became a lawyer—but that's another tale.

A few months after Daddy died, Mama moved to Nashville, Tennessee, to start the Church Recreation Service at the Baptist Sunday School Board. She and her new staff were soon publishing a newsletter that later became a quarterly magazine. She wrote books, edited story books with Clyde Maguire, and traveled throughout the South, speaking and entertaining.

She took an early retirement in 1963 and returned to her birthplace of Palmetto, Florida. She bought an old log house that she spruced up and enlarged. For a while she was minister to senior adults at the First Baptist Church of Palmetto. Then she retired from that job, but still she was an inspirational speaker in much demand. Her charisma drew people like a magnet. People listened to her, believed in her, and loved her. Many lives were touched and changed by coming into contact with her. She was booked for engagements a year in advance when she died in 1985 at the age of 85.

Many years earlier, Daddy had asked her to stay at home and raise the girls. "You'll have plenty of time after the girls are grown to spread your wings," he said. How prophetic! That is what she did. But as she looked back over her long, productive life, she said an amazing thing. "The happiest years of my life were those I spent raising my family in Eagle Rock."

Erected 1923

Eagle Rock Baptist Church
Eagle Rock, Virginia

1st Grade   *2nd Grade*   *4th Grade*

"Me and My Brother, Jimmy"
Massanetta Springs

Massanetta Springs

At Our Back Door

8th birthday

The Church and Our Garage at the Bottom of the Hill

Bill, Miss Lucy, and Frank Simmons

Our House

Our School

Main Street, Eagle Rock, 1992

The author, Lake Pylant Monhollon.

The illustrator, George Ann Brock, is a wife, mother, grandmother, and former Hallmark artist. She lives in Ellenton, Florida.

OTHER BOOKS BY THE AUTHOR

❏ *A child asks...What Does Dying Mean?*
A children's picture book explaining death from a Christian perspective, using the imagery of an earthsuit/spacesuit. Written in language simple enough for a four-year-old to understand, this book will reassure children of all ages in the face of death.
Hardcover, $14.95

❏ *The God Flow: Spiritual Living in a Physical World*
A non-threatening, natural way to share your faith with secular thinkers. Other topics that tie into that approach: Ambition and Achievement; When It Seems that God Does Not Answer Our Prayers; Finding God's Will; The Two-Dimensional Day; Living with Imperfection; Growing Older and Stronger.
Trade Paperback,116 pages, $5.95.

OTHER BOOKS FROM REFLECTION PUBLISHING COMPANY

❏ *Divine Invasion* by Michael L. Monhollon.
A fictional biography of Jesus Christ, the man who has become the reference point by which we measure time itself. "Wonderfully done...One of the top 10 Christian novels of the year." Booklist
Hardcover, 340 pages, $21.95

❏ *Gee Whiz...I'm Old!* by Agnes D. Pylant
A timeless Christan classic exploring the joys and trials of failing to die young. Contains many a laugh...also abounds in sound and helpful philosophy.
Hardcover, 64 pages, $9.95

❏ *Threescore & Ten...Wow!* by Agnes D. Pylant
Especially for anyone in their latter 60's on up who wants to remain useful. "Combines a deep faith, seventy lively years, and a great sense of humor."
Hardcover, 64 pages, $9.95

❏ *So Run Your Race:An Athlete's View of God,*
Patsy Neal
Free-verse poetry expressing the grace and power of God in touching the emotional and spiritual dimensions of the athlete.
Trade paperback, 64 pages, $9.95

❏ *Psalms & Proverbs on the Playing Field,*
Patsy Neal
Selected Psalms & Proverbs, illustrated with over 90 sports photos.
Trade Paperback, 128 pages, $9.95

Order Form

* Fax orders: (915) 690-1875

☎ Telephone orders: Toll Free: 1-888-677-0101.
Send check with order or we will bill you.

* On-line orders: www. reflectionpublishing.com
Or Amazon.com or e-mail: lakepm@msn.com

✉ Postal orders: Reflection Publishing
1 Hendrick Drive
Abilene, TX 79602
Tel: (915) 692-9651

**Please send the following books
 (see previous pages):**

_____
_____
_____
_____
_____

I understand that I may return any books for a full refund for any reason, no questions asked.

Name: _____

Address: _____

City: _____ State: _____ Zip: _____

Telephone: (_____) _____

Sales tax:
Please add 8.25% for books shipped to Texas addresses.
Shipping:
$3.00 for the first book and $2.00 for each additional book.

Call toll free and order now

Order Form

* Fax orders: (915) 690-1875

☎ Telephone orders: Toll Free: 1-888-677-0101.
Send check with order or we will bill you.

* On-line orders: www.reflectionpublishing.com
Or Amazon.com or e-mail: lakepm@msn.com

✉ Postal orders: Reflection Publishing
1 Hendrick Drive
Abilene, TX 79602
Tel: (915) 692-9651

Please send the following books
    (see previous pages):

_____
_____
_____
_____
_____
_____

I understand that I may return any books for a full refund for any reason, no questions asked.

Name: _____

Address: _____

City: _____ State: _____ Zip: _____

Telephone: (_____) _____

Sales tax:
Please add 8.25% for books shipped to Texas addresses.
Shipping:
$3.00 for the first book and $2.00 for each additional book.

Call toll free and order now